Growing
GREEN

FREE-RANGE FARMING

by Trina Mickelson

LERNER PUBLICATIONS · MINNEAPOLIS

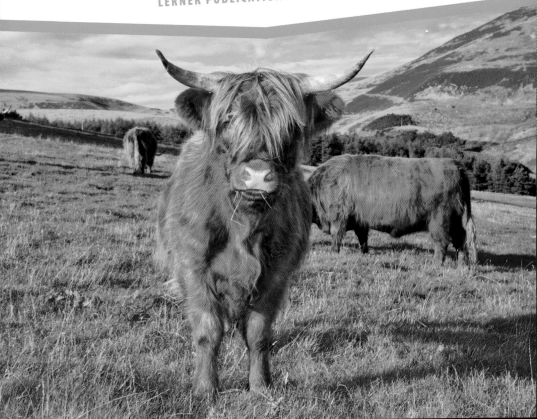

Copyright © 2016
by Lerner Publishing Group, Inc.

Content Consultant: Louise Calderwood, Sterling College,
Craftsbury Common, Vermont

Lerner Publications Company
A division of Lerner Publishing Group, Inc.
241 First Avenue North
Minneapolis, MN 55401 USA

For reading levels and more information, look up this title at
www.lernerbooks.com.

Library of Congress Cataloging-in-Publication Data

The Cataloging-in-Publication Data for *Free-Range Farming* is on file
at the Library of Congress.

ISBN 978-1-4677-9389-6 (lib. bdg.)
ISBN 978-1-4677-9710-8 (EB pdf)

Manufactured in the United States of America
1 – VP – 12/31/15

Table of

CONTENTS

FARMING MOVES INDOORS

When most people hear the word *farm*, a certain image often comes to mind. A rambling farmhouse stands in the middle of green fields. A few cows graze in the pasture while chickens scratch the dirt by a henhouse. Pigs doze in a barn or outside in the sunshine. Farm animals that are allowed to move around freely and eat what they choose are said to be "free-range" livestock.

From the dawn of agriculture until the middle of the last century, this was a typical farm setting. A small herd of cows could graze on fresh grass and clover. Cows thrive on these foods, which are inedible to people. Cows then provide milk, which people can drink. Bulls or older cows may be butchered for meat.

After a few months in one pasture, the farmer would typically move the cows to another pasture. Then the pigs took over the first field. They turned up the soil with their strong snouts, revealing a feast of roots and insects. Pigs are omnivores, so they enjoy many foods. Pigs can even eat cow dung. Then chickens went into the field, finding insects to eat in the turned-up

Many people imagine farms as places where animals are free to roam.

soil and depositing their own waste. Chicken manure is high in nitrates, which helps the grass grow thick and lush. Then the cows returned the following year to graze the fresh grass that grew in the fertilized soil.

The different plants and animals worked together. Animals ate foods that people do not eat, such as grass and insects. The animal manure

Before farming moved largely indoors, most cows spent their days grazing in grass fields.

became fertilizer, which helped new grass grow. This made an efficient loop with little waste left over. Farm animals had space, some freedom of movement, and usually enough food. They provided milk and eggs, and eventually meat, to their farmers and local people. Variations on this system worked successfully for thousands of years around the world. However, rapid population growth in the twentieth century made it difficult for farmers to grow enough food to feed everyone. New technology has helped them to raise more and larger animals on the same amount of land. But not everyone agrees that these new practices are the best choice.

Animal Feeding Operations

Farming in the United States went through major changes in the middle of the twentieth century. With the development of mechanized equipment, farms grew in size and began to specialize in raising one type of animal. Sometimes they even specialize in animals in one phase of their life, such as piglets from birth to weaning. This specialization allows farmers to provide individualized housing, feed, and veterinary care for each stage of an animal's life. Many of these animal feeding operations (AFOs) have a full-time veterinarian on staff to ensure animals receive medical attention.

AFOs can protect animals and farmers from certain threats. When animals live on a pasture, they are exposed to predators and parasites. Animals and the farmers caring for them can be injured during mating and as mothers protect their young. AFO animals do not go out into fields to graze; instead, they are kept in pens or cages, often indoors, and fed grain, primarily corn and soy. The US Environmental Protection Agency (EPA) defines these small areas as confined spaces.

AFOs, sometimes called factory farms, are an efficient way to produce a lot of meat, milk, and eggs without requiring a lot of land to house livestock. It costs less to house and feed the animals because the farmers don't need to buy and maintain large pastures. Grain feed is also cheap because the US government offers subsidies, or money grants, to farmers who grow corn and soy, which keeps prices low. AFOs have helped make these products an affordable part of an everyday diet for many Americans.

AFOs with a very large number of animals are called concentrated animal feeding operations (CAFOs). The number of animals that makes the

Case In ℞ POINT
THE VALUE OF CORN

The US government has paid subsidies to farmers since the 1930s. The goal of subsidies is to take some of the risk out of farming. If weather, disease, or insects destroy crops, the farmer still gets paid. If crop prices drop low, the farmer is not forced out of business. In 1980, payments increased and affected the way farmers plant crops. The government pays subsidies for grain crops, such as corn and soy, but not for fruits and vegetables. Many more farmers started growing corn and soy. As of 2014, instead of direct payments, farmers get free crop insurance. They can receive insurance payments to partially protect their income when the price of their crops, or their income, drops below a certain mark. Farmers who grow fruit and vegetables receive other types of help, but not the same crop insurance. This still encourages farmers to plant corn and soy.

Chickens feed at a CAFO. The United States has nearly 10,000 CAFOs.

operation a CAFO depends on the type of animal. For example, a CAFO has at least 700 dairy cows, 2,500 swine, or 125,000 broiler chickens. These animals are kept on a small area of land. Because CAFOs hold so many animals, they produce more than one-half of the meat Americans eat. Most of the United States' milk and eggs also come from CAFOs.

AFOs and CAFOs can produce larges quantities of food in small spaces and at low costs. Thanks to the inexpensive meat produced at AFOs and CAFOs, meat consumption has increased. On average, Americans eat almost

4 pounds (1.8 kilograms) of meat per week, 1 pound (0.5 kg) more per week than in the 1950s. However, not all people agree AFOs are the best methods for raising livestock. Because so many animals are housed together, farmers administer antibiotics to keep diseases at bay. They also feed animals hormones to speed up growth.

The production of cheap meat has also had some negative side effects. Some people consider AFOs to be cruel to animals. Beef cattle spend approximately six months grazing in pastures. For the rest of their lives, they are housed in feedlots, where they are fed specialized diets for rapid growth. Without grass cover, the pens can become muddy and manure soaked during rainstorms. Breeding pigs may spend years in pens called gestation crates. The cages are designed to protect newborn piglets from their large mothers, who may accidentally lay on them. The sows cannot turn around and can take only one or two steps forward and backward.

Although the stress of predation and herd behavior is removed when animals are housed in AFOs, crowded conditions can lead to stress for the animals, causing unnatural behavior. Chickens, turkeys, and ducks may fight or pull out their own feathers. To prevent this, farmers cut off parts of their beaks. They may also be housed in small cages, which prevent fighting but limit the birds' movement.

Pollution Problems

CAFOs produce approximately 300 million tons (272 million metric tons) of manure each year. That is twice the waste excreted by the entire US human population. In the right amounts, manure is useful for fertilizing fields. However, it contains several pollutants that are dangerous in high amounts.

These pollutants include ammonia, nitrogen, and phosphorus. If these substances run off into rivers or lakes, they can cause aquatic plants to grow too quickly and then die. This reduces the oxygen in the water and can kill fish and other aquatic animals. Ammonia also gets into the air, where it can irritate the lungs and eyes of people and animals.

Breeding pigs at this AFO stand in individual gestation crates. The EPA estimates that there are approximately 450,000 AFOs in the United States.

Fertilizing fields with manure is a cost-effective way to reduce waste, but it must be applied in the right amounts or else runoff can cause pollution.

Because manure can cause pollution if not managed correctly, CAFOs must adhere to strict federal regulations. For example, manure must be properly stored and applied. Farmers must also take steps to stop manure from being washed into nearby waterways by rain runoff. However, accidents from mismanaging manure have created water quality and human health problems. Manure from hog farms has accidentally leaked waste into rivers, killing thousands of fish. Some runoff has made it to the ocean, creating dead zones where fish can no longer live. Water and air pollution from large-scale farms also take a toll on human health. In some

Case In POINT

FIGHTING POLLUTION

Farmers are exempt from many of the rules other industries have to follow. Farmers and ranchers have exceptions to the Clean Air Act, the Clean Water Act, and the Safe Drinking Act. This can cause problems in the areas around AFOs and CAFOs. For example, Cow Palace LLC is a dairy farm in Granger, Washington. According to a report released in 2015, its 11,000 cows produced 40 million gallons (151 million liters) of liquid manure each year. Washing the cows produced another 61 million gallons (231 million L) of water contaminated by manure. Some of this manure and water was sprayed on fields as fertilizer. The rest was dumped into lagoons. Experts claim the lagoons leaked millions of gallons of waste into the area's soil and groundwater. Nearby wells had high levels of nitrates, which can cause serious health problems, including cancer. Cow Palace and other dairy CAFOs were sued for causing a public health threat. Lawsuits such as these, if successful, may change the rules for factory farms. If factory farms have to pay for the pollution they cause, they will no longer be able to produce animal products so cheaply. Free-range products will not seem so expensive in comparison. That will encourage more farmers to use healthy free-range practices.

Laws regulate the amount of fertilizer and manure runoff that large-scale farms can release into the environment.

instances, living within 3 miles (4.8 kilometers) of a CAFO increases health problems. Those who work at the farms have the highest health risks. Sicknesses associated include breathing trouble in the form of asthma and chronic bronchitis. CAFO workers may be exposed to dangerous chemicals, such as ammonia. Even small amounts of ammonia cause eye irritation and breathing problems. Other dangers include slippery floors, dangerous equipment, and high noise levels.

In 2015, a coalition sued the EPA for failing to properly address farm air pollution. Family farmer Rosie Partridge said, "When the emissions are at their worst, we have had to leave our home for days at a time. The ammonia and hydrogen sulfide are so strong that my husband has trouble breathing." Groundwater has been tainted by waste in many rural areas, making the local water unsafe to drink. As farmers have become aware of the dangers

To Your
HEALTH

AVOIDING POLLUTED WATER

The public water supply is tested for contaminants each year. Contaminants can come from nature or from pollution caused by humans. Many local water suppliers send information to customers once per year. This report includes information on what is in the local water and shows health risks. Some states also post online information about any problems. People who do not get public water should have their wells, or private water supply, tested every year. Even if you have public water, you can have your own tests conducted. Your family might consider testing if you observe a change in the color, smell, or taste of your water. Another reason to test is if your family or neighborhood has unexplained illnesses. If you are concerned about your water, suggest that your family start using filtered water. Instead of buying bottled water, which produces huge amounts of waste, ask your family to get a water filter for your tap. Make sure it filters out the contaminants specific to your local water.

of mismanaging manure, they have spent millions of their own dollars, combined with state and federal funds, to build structures and develop and follow plans to appropriately use manure.

Manure can even become a valuable resource. Stored manure gives off methane gas. Methane gas is a renewable energy source that can be used to produce electricity. However, if methane gas is allowed to escape into the atmosphere, it becomes a greenhouse gas and contributes to global warming.

Finding a Better Way

In contrast to AFOs, free-range livestock farming is an attempt to return to a healthier, balanced way of raising meat. On free-range farms, livestock is raised outdoors or in large pens with a comfortable layer of straw. The animals have access to fresh air and water. Typically, they are not given

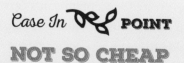

Case In POINT
NOT SO CHEAP

Although meat from AFOs may be less expensive than free-range meat, it has hidden costs. Taxpayer money pays for the subsidies to farmers. More public tax money helps pay for the disposal of manure. When manure poisons land or water, the pollution must be cleaned up, again funded by taxes. The US Department of Agriculture (USDA) estimates the total cost of proper manure disposal at $1.16 billion or more per year. Farmers spend millions of dollars annually to develop responsible and innovative approaches to manure management.

Cattle graze around a manure digester system, a round building containing machinery that captures methane and processes manure safely.

hormones, and they receive antibiotics only when they are sick, which is not often. In these circumstances, animals behave more naturally. For example, chickens are less likely to fight each other or pull out their own feathers.

On free-range farms, livestock either has access to or lives outdoors.

There are risks involved, though. The animals may be subject to other dangers, such as attacks from wild animals.

Free-range products can be more expensive than factory farm products. However, those who practice free-range farming see it as better for the animals, the people, and the land. Jerome and Nancy Kohlberg, owners of Cabbage Hill Farm in New York, take pride in their free-range animals, saying, "They breed and birth naturally, they roam and graze on pastures, and do not need antibiotics or hormones or chemically fertilized fields. Compost and manure are returned to the fields to enrich the soil. . . . There is no wasted water in this setup." People who support free-range farming say it is kinder, healthier, and better for the environment. Consumers who buy free-range meat, eggs, and milk help support these farms.

ANTIBIOTICS AND MEAT

Antibiotics are important medicines that can save lives, but only if they work. On many farms, animals are given antibiotics at low dosages for long periods. This helps prevent disease, but low-dose antibiotics can allow some germs to survive. The germs then grow resistant to antibiotics. The antibiotics may no longer cure infections as effectively. The US Centers for Disease Control and Prevention (CDC) calls antibiotic-resistant germs a serious health threat. It is much safer to only treat individual animals when they become sick. Although animals usually are given different types of antibiotics from the ones people receive, all unnecessary antibiotic use contributes to germs evolving resistance.

The European Union banned the use of most growth-promoting antibiotics (GPAs) in 1999. The goal was to keep human drugs effective. Many US animal producers are concerned that costs will go up if they stop using GPAs. However, studies suggest that is not true. The cost of the antibiotics offsets the benefits of fast-growing animals. The final word is not yet in. After a ban on most antibiotics in Denmark, overall antibiotic use decreased, but more antibiotics were used to treat animals that were sick with specific diseases. Reducing the amount of GPAs used on farms led to an increase in the number of sick animals. To successfully avoid using antibiotics, other healthy farming practices are needed. For example, giving animals more space and proper airflow can reduce disease transmission.

WHAT IS FREE-RANGE FARMING?

In her book *Harvest for Hope*, primatologist and anthropologist Jane Goodall profiled a Washington State farmer. George Vojkovich started farming with typical modern methods. He used artificial fertilizers and pesticides to improve soil and kill pests. At age forty-four, he began having irregular heart rhythms. His doctor believed this was caused by chemical exposure. Vojkovich stopped using chemicals on his farm and began allowing his animals access to the outdoors and natural foods. Now he raises free-range beef cattle, pigs, chickens, and turkeys. He lets all of his animals graze in pastures and does not give them hormones or antibiotics. These are the basics of free-range farming. Animals raised in this way take a year longer to grow than factory farm animals. But the meat Vojkovich produced won prizes for flavor. Plus, Vojkovich's heart returned to its normal rhythm.

Free-range animals are allowed to live and graze outdoors.

The chain had discovered that one of its pork suppliers was not treating pigs properly. The company's communications director, Chris Arnold, was interviewed by the *Washington Post*. He said, "This is fundamentally an animal welfare decision and it's rooted in our unwillingness to compromise our standards where animal welfare is concerned."

Large chain restaurants that demand humane animal products give farmers an incentive to use humane standards. If restaurants and their customers are willing to pay more for meat raised to these standards, more farmers and ranchers will start providing it.

Supporting Free-Range Farms

Many consumers shop based on price: they pick up the cheapest pack of chicken or the eggs on sale. However, a growing number of people also consider ethics. They are willing to pay more for food that is raised according to certain standards. Some also prefer free-range food for health or environmental reasons.

Customers who ask for humane products and are willing to pay higher prices encourage businesses to make changes. Community sponsored agricultural (CSA) programs help people buy local food directly from a farmer. Buying directly from a farmer can keep the costs low for the consumer, whereas more of the money goes to the farmer. More than 1,000 CSAs operate in the United States. Although many focus on fruits and vegetables, some provide eggs, dairy products, and meat. This can offer support to small farmers while helping consumers find the products they want at a reasonable cost.

Many Choices

The number of true free-range farms is hard to identify. The United States has thousands of small farms, but not all of these use free-range practices. When it comes to producing animal products, it is not a simple choice between confinement farming and an ideal of free-range farming where happy animals frolic in nature. Producers have many choices about how to run their businesses. For example, animals may be raised in cages, cage free, or free range. Free-range poultry producers must allow their birds access to the outdoors. This could be a grassy field or merely an area of

More and more consumers are opting for organic meat, meaning it hasn't been exposed to pesticides, fertilizers, antibiotics, or growth hormones.

gravel surrounded by fence. Cage-free animals are not raised in cages, but they might be kept in an enclosed barn. They do not necessarily get fresh air, sunshine, or space to roam. Free-range and cage-free chickens may still have their beaks cut off. Pastured chickens are allowed to forage outside. They may eat grass, seeds, worms, and so forth, in addition to grain. This may be closest to what most people imagine free range means.

Vegetarian-fed animals eat only plant products. Cows naturally have a vegetarian diet of grass, flowering plants, and leaves. Animals tend to be healthier if they are raised on their natural diet. For example, mad cow disease is thought to have come from cattle that were fed meat and bone, which are not part of their natural diet. However, vegetarian-fed cows could still be fed corn and soy, which are not part of their natural diet and cause them to get sick more often. Bugs and grubs are naturally part of a chicken's diet. Vegetarian-fed chickens are not allowed to go outside to forage.

On the other hand, confined animals grow large enough for market quicker than free-range animals do. In addition, animals raised in confinement are fed materials left over from making sugar, beer, corn syrup, cotton, and other food and products. These leftover materials would likely end up in landfills if they were not consumed by farm animals.

What Is "Organic"?

Organic products are often considered the healthiest option for people and the environment. Organic crops are grown without using most pesticides or synthetic fertilizers. For animals to be organic, they must eat only organic feed. Their food cannot have been grown with chemical fertilizers or pesticides. The animals cannot receive antibiotics or growth hormones.

Animals in confinement are fed leftover materials, such as this dried and pelleted citrus pulp, helping recycle materials otherwise put in landfills.

Organic chickens also must be free range. To use the label *organic*, companies must prove their product meets government standards.

The USDA has legal definitions for many food-labeling terms. The USDA is also responsible for making sure claims about meat and poultry products are true. Besides the USDA, some nonprofit organizations certify food. These organizations tend to focus on practices that are humane and healthy for people and the environment. The "Animal Welfare Approved"

Case In POINT

LABEL LINGO

The following labels are used to market animal products to people who consider animal welfare or human health when buying products:

- **Free-range** producers must allow their animals some sort of access to the outdoors.

- **Cage-free** animals are not raised in cages, but they can be kept in an enclosed barn.

- **Pastured** is not a legally defined term. It suggests the animal was allowed to forage, or browse for its own food outdoors, but different companies can use it to mean different things.

- **Vegetarian-fed** animals only eat plant products. Vegetarian-fed chickens are not allowed to go outside to forage for bugs.

- **Grass-fed** cattle are raised in grass pastures, but they may be moved to a feedlot for the last months of their lives.

- **Grass-finished** beef comes from cattle that spend their entire lives foraging in pastures.

- **Natural** meat means nothing was added to the meat after slaughter. The animals may still receive hormones or antibiotics while alive. They might have been fed grains grown with chemical fertilizers and pesticides. The USDA considers all eggs natural, so the term means nothing when applied to eggs.

- **Organic** products are not exposed to most pesticides, synthetic fertilizers, antibiotics, and growth hormones. The USDA mandates certain living conditions for organic livestock. They must have access to pasture, shade, and indoor shelter, for example.

label requires that animals have continual access to the outdoors. Slaughter practices must also follow certain rules. Antibiotics can be administered only to sick animals after other treatments have failed. "Certified Humane Raised and Handled" and "American Grassfed" have similar guidelines.

A USDA agent checks in on a slaughterhouse to ensure that it meets standards for humane handling of animals.

READING MEAT LABELS

If you are concerned about the humane treatment of animals, how can you know which foods to buy? Read and understand labels. Organic products are a good option for humane, healthy standards. A "Certified Organic" seal shows that the food producer has been inspected and meets organic standards, including basic standards of humane practices for livestock. If you cannot find organic meat, eggs, and dairy products, look for "Animal Welfare Approved," "Certified Humane Raised and Handled," or "American Grassfed" labels.

These organizations check that farmers using their labels are following their rules.

To some extent, free-range practices are left to farmers' choices. A farmer could use the label *grass fed* and still give the animals other foods in addition to grass. A free-range animal might have full access to the outdoors or almost no access at all. Farmers may consider a variety of factors when making a decision about how to raise animals. Concerns about animal welfare, human health, and the environment must be balanced with costs, marketing options, and following government rules.

BENEFITS OF ANIMAL WELFARE

Those who promote free-range farming say it is better for people, animals, and the environment. It is hard to know for certain whether an animal is happy because animals cannot express themselves through words. Looking for signs of agitation can be a way to judge whether an animal is unhappy.

Stress-free animals are able to produce meat, milk, and eggs efficiently. Another measure of happiness could be whether the animal has the chance to behave in a natural manner. Does the chicken get to act like a chicken, scratching in the earth for worms and seeds? Does the cow get to walk in the sunshine, grazing on grass? These activities are more in tune with their natural behavior than living in tiny enclosures. Free-range farming is a way to allow the animals to live more naturally. They get to roam outside and find some of their own food.

One sign of comfortable, stress-free chickens is high egg production.

USING YOUR CONSUMER POWER

Everyone can make a difference in how animals are treated. You can:

- Encourage your family to buy products from animals that were raised humanely.

- Shop at farmers' markets or buy meat, eggs, and milk from small local producers. Be sure to ask questions about their products. Some farmers' markets only allow the sale of local organic products. Others have no restrictions on what can be sold.

- Understand what labels mean and help shop for the right labels. If your local grocery does not carry the items you want, ask for them.

- Look for other ways to save money so your family can afford the higher-priced organic items.

- Eat at restaurants that have good policies covering where they get their ingredients. Write to your favorite restaurants asking them to consider animal welfare.

- Sign petitions and write letters to politicians supporting farm animal rights.

In the end, meat animals will be killed—an act some find cruel regardless of how well the animals live. Yet most farm animals would not be able to survive in the wild. They benefit from a relationship with humans who provide food and protection. People might cut short that life by butchering the animal for food, but in the wild, an animal's life would likely be even shorter. Animals raised for meat end their lives healthy and pain free, rather than dying from disease, predation, or the natural aging process. Dr. Temple Grandin notes, "None of the cattle [at a] slaughter plant would have been born if people had not bred and raised them. They would never have lived at all. People forget that nature can be very harsh,

Case In POINT
BISON RETURN

One animal raised for meat that is virtually always free range is the bison. More than 20 million wild bison once roamed the American West. They were nearly destroyed by hunting and the destruction of habitat. By 1899, only approximately 1,000 of these animals remained in North America. The US and Canadian governments worked to protect and increase bison herds. Today, approximately 4,500 bison live in the wild. Another 500,000 are being raised for meat in Canada and the United States. Americans eat meat from approximately 50,000 bison per year. This is a small number compared with the meat from 90,000 cattle Americans consume every day. Still, bison is the fastest-growing part of the meat business. Ranchers care for bison because their meat is worth money. This has helped save the species, and more bison are also being released into the wild.

Cattle await slaughter at a meatpacking plant.

and death in the wild is often more painful and stressful than death in a modern plant."

The treatment of animals in slaughterhouses varies greatly. In the worst slaughterhouses, animals are sometimes cut apart while still alive and conscious, which violates federal law. Animals may scream and thrash in pain and fear. In contrast, humane slaughter minimizes animal stress and suffering before slaughter. When cattle are brought to slaughterhouses, they are herded through a chute, or path, to be slaughtered. Humane chutes are designed so that cattle cannot see the impending slaughter up ahead. This helps keep the animals calm until the very end.

Dr. Grandin has designed slaughterhouse machinery. Her goal is to be humane to the animals. She wondered whether cattle knew they were going to be slaughtered as they went through the humane system she designed at the National Beef Plant. She watched them getting fed, getting their shots, and going up the ramp at the slaughter plant. She observed no difference in the cattle's behavior, noting that the cows would show obvious signs of agitation if they knew. This suggests that raising and even slaughtering animals humanely can eliminate fear and pain in animals.

Health Rewards

Proponents of free-range farming also claim free-range animals are healthier. They get sunlight and fresh air. They are not subjected to crowded conditions, which can cause disease to spread. Therefore, free-range animals do not need many antibiotics. And healthier animals may mean more healthful meat. Pastured chicken and cows get exercise, and organically raised animals are not fed hormones. This produces meat with less fat and fewer calories. The meat of animals that eat grass also has more vitamins than meat from animals that eat more grain. According to Dr. Rekha Mankad, grass-fed beef may benefit heart health more than other types of beef do. Grass-fed beef may have less total fat, more healthy fats,

Case In ⟡ POINT

URBAN CHICKENS

People in urban areas are also choosing to raise free-range meat. Raising livestock animals at home provides the freshest products with little damage to the environment. For most people, chickens are the easiest animals to raise. Some cities have laws against keeping chickens within city limits, but the practice is legal in many places.

Many urban farmers raise chickens for their eggs, to eat at home or to sell at local farmers' markets. They may also eventually butcher the chickens for meat. In some places, mobile slaughterhouses visit the neighborhood to handle the butchering. Keeping hens in the backyard comes with challenges. Pets or wild animals can kill the birds. Hens can live for years after they stop producing eggs. Owners who do not want to kill their birds for meat must keep a chicken that is not giving eggs.

and more antioxidant vitamins. Little study has been done on long-term benefits of eating grass-fed beef, however.

Free-range farming can also be healthier for the land. Allowing animals to graze in reasonable numbers helps maintain grasslands. Trees and shrubs do not take over areas that were naturally grasslands. In fact, some states bring in sheep or goats to graze in areas where nonnative plant species have taken over. This helps restore natural wildlife habitat. Letting animals graze in former farm fields can allow the land to return to natural prairie. Cows fertilize the soil with their manure and spread seeds with their hooves. When farm fields are replaced by grazing grasslands, soil erosion decreases dramatically. However, free-range farming takes a lot of land. The United States must balance its need for more land for homes and cities with its need for farming and raising animals and its desire to leave some lands wilderness.

Balancing Benefits

Proponents of CAFO systems claim CAFO practices produce and provide meat at lower costs. This may turn out to be a myth. Several studies have compared pasture-raised or organic meat, milk, and egg production to CAFO systems. The methods were similar in both farming costs and the amount of food produced. Dairy cattle raised in pastures produce less milk, but they need much less grain. Not needing to buy grain saves farmers money. Dairy cows raised on free-range farms can be allowed to graze in pastures, changing pastures often, with less environmental damage.

Hog hoop barns use fabric on metal arches, with deep beds of straw for bedding. Animals usually have more space and freedom of movement and

Cattle rest in a hoop barn, an alternative to small pens, at an AFO.

may have access to the outdoors. Hoop barns are cheaper to install than traditional CAFO buildings and cost approximately the same to maintain. An Iowa State University study compared tiny pig gestation crates with hoop barns where animals could move around and socialize. Hoop barns turned out to be slightly cheaper. Studies such as these show free-range farming can be both humane and cost effective.

CHALLENGES OF CHANGE

The idea of animals living peacefully in nature is appealing. In reality, giving animals open access to nature brings a host of problems. For example, pastured animals are exposed to heat, cold, wind, and snow. Free-range egg farmer Forrest Pritchard described one harsh winter: "I spent my winter shoveling my chickens out of snow drifts, thawing frozen waterlines with a hair dryer, and gathering eggs hourly so they didn't freeze and burst." Predators such as foxes, raccoons, and hawks may attack. A large flock of chickens damages a grassy area in a few days. They may lay their eggs in hidden areas that are hard to find. Even free-range chickens can get sick and must be treated.

While predation is not as much of an issue for larger livestock, cattle and other large animals also face issues of harsh weather conditions and exposure to parasites. For example, low rainfall amounts and extreme heat can deter grass growth. This leaves grazing animals, such as cows, with little to eat. Free-range pigs are exposed to more parasites, such as worms and

Free-range chickens are more likely to be attacked by their natural predators, such as foxes.

Chicken coops are one form of protection from natural elements and predators.

lice. Infestations can affect how much food the pigs are eating, which then slows their growth and breeding rates.

Free-range farming can mean a lot more work for farmers. For example, very few chickens are raised with fully free-range practices. It is easier to keep chickens confined in buildings that can be heated and cooled. Medical care for large herds or flocks is also a challenge. It is simpler to give a large group of animals antibiotics than to watch for sick animals and treat each one individually.

Still, free-range challenges can be managed. For example, a chicken coop can protect chickens from the weather. Electrified nets keep out predators. The birds can be moved to a new grazing area every few days, giving the depleted area time to recover. Natural treatments, such as garlic and chilies in place of antibiotics, can help the birds stay healthy.

But there are limits to how many people can be fed meat through ideal free-range practices. The US population is growing. If every American eats meat several times per day, there will not be enough grassland to support the number of farm animals needed. Some meat is imported from other countries, but that practice causes additional problems. For

Case In POINT

NEW METHODS

One challenge of implementing free-range practices is the change farmers must accept. Dr. Grandin has helped develop more humane methods of handling farm animals. She bases her methods and equipment on studies of animal behavior. However, she has found it difficult to convince the agricultural industry to use these methods. She notes, "Some people will purchase a new cattle-handling system, which is designed with animal behavioral principles, but they will continue to handle cattle roughly.

People are more willing to purchase new equipment than they are to use easy-to-learn, low-stress handling techniques. Even when financial benefits are clear, some people find it difficult to believe that a behavioral management method really works."

example, huge areas of rain forest have been replaced with grazing land for cattle. Producing less meat may be the best option for protecting the environment, but that requires millions of people changing their eating habits.

The Cost of Meat

Free-range meat can cost two or three times as much as meat from animals housed in confinement. This higher cost makes it hard for some

Large areas of the Amazon Rainforest in Brazil have been burned and cut down to make room for cattle to graze.

DEMANDING MORE MEAT

Large farms are both a result and a cause of our growing demand for meat. Overall, people are eating more meat than ever. In 1975, Americans ate an average of 3.4 pounds (1.5 kg) of meat each week. That number has increased to more than 5 pounds (2.3 kg) per week. When dairy products and eggs are included, an average American eats more than 17 pounds (7.7 kg) of animal products per week. Americans eat more meat than almost anyone else in the world. The world average of meat consumption is approximately 1.8 pounds (0.08 kg) per week, approximately one-third of what Americans eat.

It is unlikely that small family farms with pastured animals would be able to supply all the US meat demands in the near future. However, most people eat far more meat and animal products than they need. Many health professionals recommend people reduce their intake of meat and dairy products. If people ate less meat, free-range farming practices would be better able to meet the demand.

families to afford. One study found that a family of four would have to pay approximately $63 more per week to eat an entirely organic diet, including fruits and vegetables. Some products are much more expensive if they are organic. For other products, the price difference is not that large, and a few organic products may even be cheaper at times. Organic meat is likely to be more expensive, but how much more expensive varies. For example, one study found chicken and eggs to have a higher price difference than beef, pork, and turkey.

EATING LESS MEAT

Most people eat more meat than they need for good health. By eating less meat, your family may find it easier to afford free-range meat when you do eat meat. Here are some ways you can cut back:

- Try eating meat less often. You might eat meat only once per day. Or your family could decide to go without any meat on some days.

- Eat smaller portions of meat. According to the USDA, an official serving of meat is 3 to 4 ounces (85 to 113 grams). That is approximately the size of a deck of cards. Many people eat much larger servings.

- At restaurants, pack up one-half of your meat to take home for later. To avoid wasteful packaging, bring your own reusable container.

Free-range advocates point out that confinement farms have hidden costs not often taken into account. If the government stopped tax subsidies to AFOs, the two kinds of meat would cost approximately the same. People would pay lower taxes and they might also have lower health care costs. Current business practices are also hard on small-scale free-range farmers. A few very large companies control the market for slaughtering and processing meat. The largest four beef processing firms control 83.5 percent of the market. They often do not contract with small producers. This makes it difficult for small farmers to get their meat to market. Needing to travel long distances to slaughterhouses is also hard on the animals.

To cut back on meat consumption, consider making one day of the week meatless.

As with any movement, free-range farming must face some challenges. Farmers must keep free-range animals—which would otherwise be kept in buildings and treated with antibiotics—safe and healthy. Free-range farmers also face the challenge of feeding the world's population. But the many benefits of free-range farming keep this movement on the rise.

THE FUTURE OF FREE-RANGE FARMING

It is hard to find accurate numbers on the percentage of farm animals raised humanely, especially with the different definitions for what that term means. The trend seems to be growing, though, and is likely to continue. In March 2015, Compass Group USA, a large food-service company, committed to using only cage-free eggs. The company had already started using cage-free eggs for eggs sold whole in the shell in 2007. That policy affected the purchase of 48 million eggs per year. The newer policy also covered the purchase of eggs bought in liquid form. This takes an additional one million hens from tiny cages into cage-free buildings. By 2019, the companies supplying eggs to Compass must also follow Humane Farm Animal Care standards, which will be checked by an outside organization.

Use of gestation crates for hogs is also fading. Nine states have passed laws that prohibit using gestation crates. A poll found that 95 percent

Free-range farming practices are on the rise.

Many fast-food restaurants, including McDonald's, have stopped buying pork from farms that cage and pen their pigs in small crates.

of Americans believe farm animals should be well cared for and believe gestation crates are not humane. Many large food companies have promised to stop buying pork from companies that use the pens. These companies include fast-food restaurants McDonald's, Burger King, Wendy's, SUBWAY, Denny's, Jack in the Box, and Carl's Jr. Grocery stores such as Kroger, Safeway, and Costco have made the commitment, along with the producers Oscar Meyer, Heinz, and Campbell Soup. Full compliance may take some time, and pigs may still not have access to the outdoors. But in a few years, most animals may be free from tiny cages.

The Future of Meat

Some people believe the only answer to ensure proper animal welfare is for everyone to stop eating animal products. But others believe it is possible to balance humane treatment with eating meat. Many people, including Dr. Grandin, believe animals can still be used for food, and this can be done ethically. That includes giving the animals a decent life. Dr. Grandin believes many things in animal agriculture need to be corrected. She has visited places where animals are treated well. Dr. Grandin, along with other free-range farming proponents, promotes a more widespread use of these practices.

Vaclav Smil is the author of *Should We Eat Meat?: Evolution and Consequences of Modern Carnivory*. He believes that people are physically

Case In POINT

DO NO HARM?

In *The Omnivore's Dilemma*, Michael Pollan points out that even vegetarian diets can injure animals. Farm equipment, such as tractors and combines, accidentally kills small wild animals. Pesticides destroy insects, and sometimes mice, birds, and other animals. Feeding everyone on plants would require turning more wild land into farm fields, which could hurt wild animals. Without manure from farm animals to use as fertilizer, more chemical fertilizers would be needed. These chemicals can kill fish in nearby streams. Finally, if no one ate meat, farmers would have no reason to keep meat animals. Some species live only on farms; they might die out. Realistically, it is impossible for people to survive without doing some damage to the world. Still, certain choices can cause less damage.

Eating less meat would still provide all the health benefits from meat and could in fact be healthier.

designed to eat meat. It has been suggested that eating meat is one reason people developed large brains and advanced civilizations. Smil believes that people can continue to eat meat while protecting the environment and considering animal welfare. He also recommends cutting back our overall consumption of meat by approximately one-third. People who eat a lot of meat might need to cut back more. People in poor countries could then increase their consumption to healthier levels. Smil notes that this would benefit people from different incomes.

One way to encourage less consumption could be raising the price of meat. Higher prices would encourage people to eat less meat, while more accurately reflecting the true cost of producing meat. Changes to the way we raise animals for meat could benefit humans while improving treatment of animals. Smil claims that better efficiency and less waste could cut costs. Grazing animals must be kept in numbers low enough that they do not

WHY EAT MEAT?

Most people are omnivores. They eat plants, meat, and animal products such as milk and eggs. Meat is an excellent source of protein, which the body needs. Meat and other animal products are considered complete proteins, because they have all of the essential amino acids people need. Meat also has several vitamins and minerals that the body needs, such as iron, zinc, and B vitamins. Although these nutrients can be found in other foods, they may not be found in such high amounts. They can also be harder to absorb from other foods. A vegetarian diet can also be healthy, if people eat the right foods. Otherwise they may not get enough protein and certain vitamins. For example, rice and beans each contain protein and some amino acids. But eating only rice or only beans would not provide all the amino acids needed. Rice and beans can be eaten together to provide the necessary amino acids.

SAVING MONEY ON ANIMAL PRODUCTS

Some people buy meat in bulk from a local supplier. They might buy one-quarter or one-half of a cow. This provides different cuts of meat, which can be stored in a large freezer. Grass-fed beef bought this way costs close to what beef costs at the grocery store. Groups of friends may also share a full cow or portion of a cow. This practice is known as cow pooling.

Major grocery stores and retailers such as Walmart and Costco carry some free-range foods. These are likely to be cheaper than food bought at a specialty grocery store. In some cases, buying animal products from a farmers' market or directly from a local farmer may help bring the cost down. Shopping for free-range products on sale or using coupons can also help.

damage the environment. Animals can also eat waste products from crops, such as leaves and peels left over from fruits and vegetables. They can eat the parts of rice and wheat that are stripped off during processing. This disposes of those unused products, turning them into meat that people can eat.

Smil believes that these and other efficient practices could maintain adequate meat production without destroying forests or raising animals in inhumane conditions. In his view, human health, a healthy environment, animal welfare, and reasonable costs can all happen together.

Many government regulations could do a better job supporting smaller farms and humane practices. The Union of Concerned Scientists (UCS) recommends that the government stop policies that support CAFOs. Instead, the group recommends policies that support alternative farming methods. Stricter enforcement of the Clean Water Act at CAFOs could reduce the problems with manure. Changes to the Clean Air Act could reduce air pollution. Government funding should go to research and systems that benefit public health and the environment. For example,

Feeding animals food scraps that would normally be composted can help reduce waste.

SCHOOL FOOD

A large component of the free-range farming movement is being aware about where your food comes from. Do you know where your school food comes from? Ask questions to find out. If you are not satisfied with the answer, what can you do? Perhaps a group of students, parents, and teachers can make a difference. Get advice and help from groups already working on healthy school lunches. Visit websites for Revolution Foods, The Lunch Box, the Edible Schoolyard Project, and Farm to School.

subsidies could support small farms that use humane practices. Funding could also support research into new production methods. It could focus on methods that are kind to animals while benefiting the environment and public health. Finally, CAFOs should have to pay for the harm they cause to the environment. In 2014, a new farm bill that helps set agricultural policy for the United States ushered in changes friendly to organic farmers. Funding for fruits and vegetables and organic programs are set to increase

50 percent in ten years. Other changes lessened subsidies for grain, something the UCS study had recommended two years earlier.

The free-range farming movement continues to gain awareness around the world and will likely continue to do so in the future as more and more people get interested in where their food comes from. Free-range farming proponents think the goal should be ensuring that food production systems take good care of animals. Supporting free-range farming practices is a way to do that.

How do you support your local free-range farmers?

Working as a
RANCHER

anchers work long hours and cannot take vacations without finding someone else to do the work. They do not have weekends because the animals always need attention. A rancher's day usually starts at dawn. Sometimes the job is hot or cold, muddy, or physically painful. The work is hard, but it is rewarding for people who love working with animals and the land.

Ranchers need to keep accounts of income and expenses. They also need to keep equipment maintained and track changing prices, laws, and the weather. Today's ranchers are businesspeople, and most have gone to college to study animal science. Courses in marketing and finance are also helpful.

One-half of the farmers in the United States today are likely to retire in the next decade. That leaves opportunities for young people wanting to enter farming. Programs such as the Center for Rural Affairs' Land Link help match retiring farmers with new farmers. This provides new farmers access to land, financing, and education. Government and other programs also help new ranchers and farmers buy equipment and supplies.

For Catherine Friend, author of *The Compassionate Carnivore*, ranching is also about raising animals healthily and humanely. Friend and her partner raise sheep on a small farm. She believes that "Treating animals with respect and consideration is an act that sends out ever-widening ripples into the world."

GLOSSARY

antibiotic: a drug that is used to kill harmful bacteria and cure infections

groundwater: water found underground, held in the pores or cracks in soil, sand, or rock

hormone: a substance produced by the body that influences the way the body grows

subsidies: money, usually paid by the government, that helps a business or industry survive and keep prices low

SOURCE NOTES

15. "Coalition Sues EPA for Failing to Address Factory Farm Air Pollution," *Humane Society*, http://www.humanesociety.org/news/press_releases/2015/01/epa-lawsuit-ff-air-pollution-012815.html.

18. Jane Goodall, *Harvest for Hope: A Guide to Mindful Eating* (New York: Warner Books, 2005).

25. Roberto A. Ferdman, "Why Chipotle's Pork Problem Is a Bad Sign for Its Future," *The Washington Post* (January 14, 2015), http://www.washingtonpost.com/blogs/wonkblog/wp/2015/01/14/why-chipotles-pork-problem-is-a-bad-sign-for-its-future/.

35. Temple Grandin, "Avoid Being Abstract When Making Policies on the Welfare of Animals," http://www.grandin.com/welfare/avoid.abstract.making.policy.animal.welfare.pdf.

42. Forrest Pritchard, "Support Local Farms? Then Never Do What This Guy Did," *Smith Meadows* (2015), http://smithmeadows.com/farm/support-local-farms-then-never-do-what-this-guy-did/.

45. Temple Grandin, "Transferring Results of Behavioral Research to Industry to Improve Animal Welfare on the Farm, Ranch and the Slaughter Plant," *Applied Animal Behaviour Science* 81, no. 3 (2003): 215–228.

60. Catherine Friend, *The Compassionate Carnivore* (Philadelphia, PA: Da Capo Lifelong, 2008).

SELECTED BIBLIOGRAPHY

"Animal Feeding Operations," *US Environmental Protection Agency*, http://www.epa.gov/agriculture/anafoidx.html.

Goodall, Jane. *Harvest for Hope: A Guide to Mindful Eating*. New York: Warner Books, 2005.

Grandin, Temple, "Transferring Results of Behavioral Research to Industry to Improve Animal Welfare on the Farm, Ranch and the Slaughter Plant," *Applied Animal Behaviour Science* 81, no. 3 (2003): 215–228.

Gurian-Sherman, Doug, "CAFOs Uncovered: The Untold Costs of Confined Animal Feeding Operations." Cambridge, MA: UCS Publications, 2008. http://www.ucsusa.org/sites/default/files/legacy/assets/documents/food_and_agriculture/cafos-uncovered.pdf.

Nestle, Marion. *What to Eat*. New York: North Point Press, 2006.

Pollan, Michael. *The Omnivore's Dilemma: A Natural History of Four Meals*. New York: Penguin, 2006.

FURTHER INFORMATION

American Society for the Prevention of Cruelty to Animals
http://www.aspca.org
The American Society for the Prevention of Cruelty to Animals fights cruelty to animals, including farm animals. See how you can help.

Burgan, Michael. *Making Food Choices*. Chicago: Heinemann, 2012. Explore food and eating lifestyles around the world, and read tips on how you can make good choices.

Compassion in World Farming
http://www.ciwf.com
This farm animal welfare organization shares information about the myths and reality of farm animals. Learn how you can make a difference.

Langley, Andrew. *Is Organic Food Better?* Chicago: Heinemann, 2009. Dive into the topic of organic food with case studies, reports, and discussion questions.

The Lunch Box
http://www.thelunchbox.org/
See how schools are making changes to their lunch programs, and find resources to become a junior chef.

Perdew, Laura. *Eating Local*. Minneapolis, MN: Lerner, 2016. Read about the ways in which you can eat local and why it's important to do so.

Rosen, Michael J. *Our Farm: Four Seasons with Five Kids on One Family's Farm*. Minneapolis, MN: Millbrook Press, 2012. Children share an inside view of life on a farm, including working with animals.

Rudick, Dina. *Barnyard Kids: A Family Guide for Raising Animals*. Beverly, MA: Quarry Books, 2015. Learn about raising farm animals and other fun farming activities.

USDA: Farm to School
http://www.fns.usda.gov/farmtoschool/farm-school
Find out how your school can use more local, sustainable foods.

INDEX

Photo Acknowledgments

The images in this book are used with the permission of: © SergeBertasiusPhotography/Shutterstock Images, p. 1; © TFoxFoto/Shutterstock Images, p. 5; © Vibrant Image Studio/Shutterstock Images, p. 6; © Maks Narodenko/Shutterstock Images, p. 8; © ugurerden/iStockphoto, p. 9; © Dmitry Kalinovsky/Shutterstock Images, p. 11; © Bildagentur Zoonar GmbH/Shutterstock Images, p. 12; © Lynn Betts/Natural Resources Conservation Service/US Department of Agriculture, p. 14; © CreativeNature R.Zwerver/Shutterstock Images, p. 17; © BMJ/Shutterstock Images, p. 18; © janecat/Shutterstock Images, p. 21; © Craig Lee/San Francisco Chronicle/Corbis, p. 22; © 2/Alex CaoLKL/Ocean/Corbis, p. 26; © Steve Cordory/Shutterstock Images, p. 28; © Nati Harnik/AP Images, p. 30; © carterdayne/iStockphoto, p. 33; © Eric Isselee/Shutterstock Images, p. 35; © Charlie Riedel/AP Images, p. 36; © Jennie Woodcock/Reflections Photolibrary/Corbis, p. 38; © Sterling College CC2.0, p. 40; © Phil Scarlett/iStockphoto/Thinkstock, p. 43; © Eileen Groome/iStockphoto, p. 44; © guentermanaus/Shutterstock Images, p. 46; © Spotmatik Ltd/Shutterstock Images, p. 49; © 1000 Words/Shutterstock Images, p. 51; © RiverNorthPhotography/iStockphoto, p. 52; © Jacek Chabraszewski/Shutterstock Images, p. 54; © Sharon Day/Shutterstock Images, p. 57; © Mike Flippo/Shutterstock Images, p. 58; © aimintang/iStockphoto, p. 59.

Front cover: © Laura Doss/Image Source/Getty Images (top left); © SergeBertasiusPhotography/Shutterstock.com (top right); © S-F/Shutterstock.com (bottom left); © iStockphoto.com/Jen Grantham (bottom right).